Walk Around

UH-60 Black Hawk

By Richard S. Dann

Color by Don Greer

Illustrated by Ernesto Cumpian and Richard Hudson

Walk Around Number 19

squadron/signal publications

Introduction

As an SH-60B pilot with 50 missions during the Gulf War, I have come to know and appreciate the outstanding versatility of the Black Hawk/Seahawk family of helicopters. Perhaps no military helicopter since the UH-1 Huey has been adapted for so many missions and performed all of them extremely well.

Even as this book goes to press, the Hawk family continues to grow. The Army is receiving the UH-60Q medical evacuation (MEDEVAC) helicopter, while the Navy is testing the CH-60, which will eventually replace their CH-46 vertical replenishment (VERTREP) aircraft. In the future, the Navy will also move towards a common tactical Seahawk airframe, known as the SH-60R.

Even though the Black Hawk and Seahawk bear a strong family resemblance, there are many differences between the airframes. Naval Hawks are built to withstand the rigors of operations at sea, and are equipped with state-of-the-art ASW electronics, while Army and Air Force Hawks are built for operations in the field. I will attempt to spell out these differences, as well as common systems and equipment on the different variants.

It must be stated that I have merely scratched the surface on documenting all the different variations of the Hawk family. It should also be remembered that many other nations fly Black Hawk and Seahawk airframes, but this book will focus primarily on US military variants.

Finally, I would like to thank all the people involved with this project. Special thanks go to Chris Belobrajdic, also Chris Miller and especially Sherman Collings (both of Cobra Models) for providing timely information when the project stalled. It must be stated here and now, "If it was meant to fly, it would have rotors!"

Acknowledgements

CDR Earl Gay	LTJG Pat Hanrahan	HSL-43 Battlecats
Rodd Mullett	LT Lisa Blow, USCG	CDR Terry Jones
Carol Tang	Allison Dann	Ashley Dann
Jerry Foster	Tony Bunch	HS-8 Eightballers
Pete Kover	Bill Tuttle	Sikorsky
Rainer Hanxleden	Bruce Hensel	David C. Raatz
Tracy Kreckman	Chris Belobrajdic	Jim Mashburn
Sherman Collings	Chris Miller	Andre Dyer
Victoria Lazare	James Ashpole	Jeff Merrick
Cobra Models	Dan Cencer	Eric Renth
Luis Yarro	MAJ Richard Cole, USAF	Werner Roth
Manfred Faber	P. Fiegel	Gerhard Weinmann
Jim Rotramel	The Bayview Duck	Lisa Dupuis

Thanks goes to all my shipmates from HSL-43 Det 2B, 'Dolan's Dogs'. It was a lovely cruise.
Special thanks goes to my dearest friends and modelfest buddies, Jerry Foster and Tony Bunch.

(Previous Page) A SH-60B prepares to launch from the flight deck of the USS CROMMELIN (FFG-37), which is equipped with the Recovery, Assist, Secure, and Traverse (RAST) system. The Seahawk is cleared for operations up to Sea State Five. This particular aircraft has been retrofitted with circular ALQ-156 threat warning sensors on the nose and fuselage sides. (Bruce Hensel)

ISBN 0-89747-405-8

If you have any photographs of aircraft, armor, soldiers or ships of any nation, particularly wartime snapshots, why not share them with us and help make Squadron/Signal's books all the more interesting and complete in the future. Any photograph sent to us will be copied and the original returned. The donor will be fully credited for any photos used. Please send them to:

Squadron/Signal Publications, Inc.
1115 Crowley Drive
Carrollton, TX 75011-5010

Если у вас есть фотографии самолётов, вооружения, солдат или кораблей любой страны, особенно, снимки времён войны, поделитесь с нами и помогите сделать новые книги издательства Эскадрон/Сигнал ещё интереснее. Мы переснимем ваши фотографии и вернём оригиналы. Имена приславших снимки будут сопровождать все опубликованные фотографии. Пожалуйста, присылайте фотографии по адресу:

Squadron/Signal Publications, Inc.
1115 Crowley Drive
Carrollton, TX 75011-5010

軍用機、装甲車両、兵士、軍艦などの写真を所持しておられる方はいらっしゃいませんか？どの国のものでも結構です。作戦中に撮影されたものが特に良いのです。Squadron/Signal社の出版する刊行物において、このような写真は内容を一層充実し、興味深くすることができます。当方にお送り頂いた写真は、複写の後お返しいたします。出版物中に写真を使用した場合は、必ず提供者のお名前を明記させて頂きます。お写真は下記にご送付ください。

Squadron/Signal Publications, Inc.
1115 Crowley Drive
Carrollton, TX 75011-5010

(Front Cover) A US Army UH-60A is parked on a forward airfield in Albania during the summer of 1999. The Black Hawk was participating in OPERATION JOINT FORCE, the NATO air campaign against Yugoslavia.

(Back Cover) The author's SH-60B flies alongside USS WISCONSIN (BB-64) as it fires a full broadside during OPERATION DESERT STORM. This aircraft (BuNo 162991) was one of two SH-60Bs of HSL-43 Detachment 2B which were deployed aboard USS MOBILE BAY (CG-53) between August 1990 and March 1991.

US Army UH-60A/L Black Hawk

The US Army began the H-60 Hawk family by selecting the Sikorsky UH-60A as the winner of the Utility Tactical Transport Aircraft System (UTTAS) competition during 1976. The Army has become the largest operator of Hawks in the world, receiving 974 UH-60A Black Hawks between 1979 and 1989. In late 1989, the UH-60A was succeeded in production by the UH-60L, which featured uprated engines and an improved gearbox.

UH-60 derivatives for the US Army include 22 MH-60K special operations aircraft, 66 EH-60C Quick Fix electronic warfare aircraft, and up to 120 UH-60Q Medical Evacuation (MEDEVAC) aircraft.

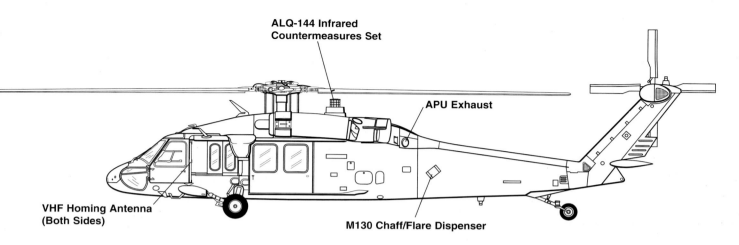

ALQ-144 Infrared Countermeasures Set

APU Exhaust

VHF Homing Antenna (Both Sides)

M130 Chaff/Flare Dispenser

A Texas Army National Guard UH-60L Black Hawk sits on the tarmac at Naval Air Station Dallas during November of 1992. Compared to the earlier UH-60A, the UH-60L features more powerful engines, an upgraded transmission, improved flight controls, and a revised tail rotor control system. This aircraft is equipped with Hover Infrared Suppressor Subsystem (HIRSS) exhaust shields, which reduce the engine IR signature in all flight profiles. (Eric Renth)

A US Army UH-60A is prepared for flight. The engine exhausts on this Black Hawk are not fitted with HIRSS shields. Between 1978 and 1989, 974 UH-60As were produced before production switched to the UH-60L. A fairing for the External Stores Support System (ESSS) mount is located in front of the cargo cabin door. The UH-60A is painted overall Helo Drab (FS34031) — the standard US Army helicopter camouflage scheme — with black lettering. (Luis Yarro)

4

Both pilots' doors are open on this California Army National Guard UH-60A (82-4747) based at Los Alamitos Army Air Field in Long Beach, California. The UH-60A/L serve with units of the Regular Army, as well as the Army Reserve and National Guard. The UH-60L is the current Army production model. (Dann)

The Black Hawk's nose bay houses secure communications equipment, an Identification Friend or Foe (IFF) system, gyroscopes, and accelerometers for the flight controls. When not in use, classified equipment is removed from the aircraft and stored in a secure area. (Dann)

Both pilots' seats in the UH-60 series are armor protected. The side armor has been extended fully forward to enclose the pilot. Black Hawk pilots sit in 'stroking' seats, which are capable of sustaining a 14g landing before the mounts compress. The left pilot's cyclic stick is placed in front of the seat. (Dann)

UH-60 Development

US Army UH-60A Black Hawk

US Air Force MH-60G Pave Hawk

US Navy SH-60B Seahawk

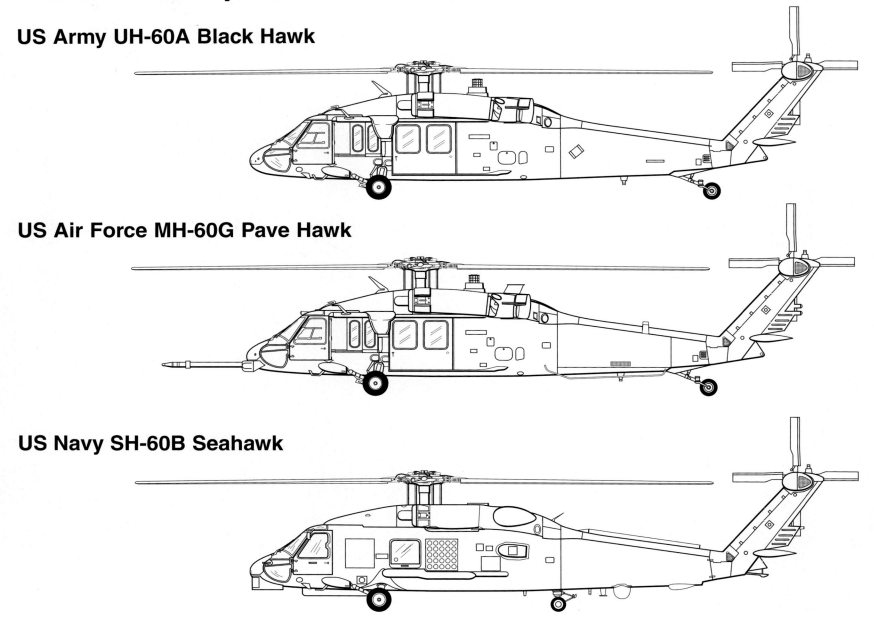

The inside of the UH-60A's port side door is equipped with a small black pouch for checklists, maps, or other small items. A circular air vent is located just under the yellow emergency exit pull handle. (Dann)

The door window of the Black Hawk features a small sliding window, which may be opened or closed from the inside. Both pilots' doors can be jettisoned in an emergency. The SH-60 Seahawk pilots' doors are not jettisonable and lack the small sliding window. (Dann)

The UH-60's circuit breakers are located above and slightly behind the pilots' seats and are separated by the overhead console. A window directly above each seat provides vertical vision for the pilot and co-pilot. A circular 'Grimes light' for use by the pilot is stowed alongside the overhead console, and may be unclipped for use in the cockpit. (Dann)

The UH-60A is equipped with analog flight instruments. This cockpit is equipped with blue lighting for night vision goggle flying. To the right of the instrument cluster is the caution, warning, and advisory panel, which has amber caution lights and green advisory lights. These lights inform the pilot of systems' status and malfunctions. (Dann)

The overhead console contains the Power Control Levers (PCLs), fuel handles, and fire 'T-handles'. These 'T-handles' arm and discharge fire extinguishing agents into the engine compartments. Auxiliary power unit controls are located aft of the PCLs. The coiled cords are attached to 'Grimes lights', which have both clear and colored lenses. (Dann)

The cyclic sticks are equipped with 'pinky triggers' in front of the grip which allow the pilot to override the flight control system and manually control the stabilator. The console between the pilots' seats contains radio communications and navigation controls. (Dann)

The starboard side of the UH-60A's instrument panel duplicates the port side's analog flight instruments. Engine pressure and temperature gauges are on the left side while the master warning panel, indicating to the pilot emergencies or abnormal situations, is located above the attitude indicator. (Dann)

(Right) The back of the pilots' seats are equipped with the crew chief's intercommunications system controls and storage for ammunition. A first aid kit is placed at the upper rear of the seat. The swiveling mount can be fitted with either a 7.62mm M60D machine gun or an M134 Minigun. A fire extinguisher is mounted on the cabin wall. (Dann)

The port collective stick is extended for the left pilot's use. To facilitate pilot entry, the collective is twisted 90° and stowed. The grip contains searchlight controls, an engine trim switch, cargo hook emergency release, and a flight control servo switch. (Dann)

The port pilot's and cabin doors are open on this UH-60A, however, the gunner's sliding windows are closed. The hydraulics bay access step is lowered in front of the cabin. A red position light is located on the main axle fairing which also incorporates a cockpit step. The starboard main axle fairing has a green position light. (Dann)

UH-60 Pilot's Seat

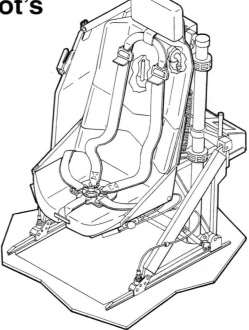

A Very High Frequency/Frequency Modulation (VHF/FM) homing antenna is mounted behind both pilots' doors. This antenna can be used to home in on a radio signal emitted from a remote source, including a soldier in the field with the appropriate communication capability. The white stenciling on the green antenna reads ANTENNA DO NOT PAINT. (Dann)

The UH-60 is capable of mounting a General Electric 7.62mm M134 Minigun, with a firing rate of 2000 to 4000 rounds per minute, in each gunner's window. A light green (believed to be FS34583) flexible shell chute is used to reduce the chances of Foreign Object Damage (FOD) to the aircraft from spent rounds. Typically, a dedicated gunner sits on the port side while the crew chief operates the other M134 in the starboard gunner's window. (Sherman Collings)

UH-60 Seat Arrangement

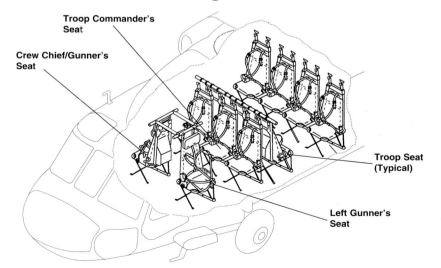

Troop Commander's Seat

Crew Chief/Gunner's Seat

Troop Seat (Typical)

Left Gunner's Seat

A UH-60L lifts an M1036 Avenger HMMWV (Highly Mobile Multipurpose Wheeled Vehicle) on a demonstration flight. The UH-60L is capable of carrying external loads of up to 9000 lbs (4082.4 KG) — 1000 lbs (453.6 KG) more than the UH-60A. This capability is due to the UH-60L's Improved Durability Gearbox and 1940 SHP General Electric T-700-GE-701C engines. (Sikorsky via Bill Tuttle)

Four troop seats line the aft cabin of this UH-60A. The back of one of the three forward-facing front row seats is at right, with the bottom of an aft-facing seat behind the front row. The Black Hawk can seat 11 fully-equipped soldiers. (Dann)

This US Customs Black Hawk is equipped with a 185 gallon (700.3 LITER) fuel bladder kit replacing the aft row of troop seats. Straps secure the fuel bladder to the aft cabin wall. Sixteen UH-60As, coming from the US Army inventory, were delivered to the US Customs Service during the latter half of the 1980s for drug interdiction missions along known smuggling routes across the southern US. (Hanxleden)

The troop seats are equipped with four-point harnesses, while the pilots' seats are equipped with five-point quick-release belts. The upper portion of the troop seats is secured to the ceiling with turnbuckles. (Dann)

The cargo hook on all Hawks is accessible through the 'hellhole' in the cabin floor. The hook is shown in the stowed position, swung 90° to starboard. This cargo hook is capable of carrying an 8000 lb (3628.8 KG) external load on the UH-60A, or a 9000 lb (4082.4 KG) load on the UH-60L. The circular objects on the cabin floor are tie down rings for internal cargo. (Dann)

The UH-60 cabin is equipped with large sliding doors on both sides of the aircraft. These doors can be open or closed in flight and have an operating limitation of 145 knots (268.7 KMH) in the open position. The interior of the aircraft is gray (FS36231) with soundproofing material being either tan or green. (Dann)

The port gunner's seat faces a closed window. The gunners' seats are anchored to the floor and are also secured to a tubular anchor in the cabin ceiling. Generally, a gunner from the infantry squad will occupy the port gunner's seat, while the Black Hawk's crew chief will occupy the starboard gunner's seat. (Dann)

The crew chief normally sits at the starboard gunner's window. The mount for a 7.62 mm M60D machine gun is located in front of the seat. The gunner can either be buckled in securely, or strap on a gunner's belt which allows more mobility in the cabin. Both the seat and gunner's belts are dark gray — approximately FS36076. (Dann)

The crew chief's M60 machine gun mount is located at the forward corner of the window. Just below the window is the external power receptacle access panel. The gunner's seat is Olive Drab (FS34087) with a tan headrest and dark gray seat belts. (Dann)

UH-60A/L Black Hawk

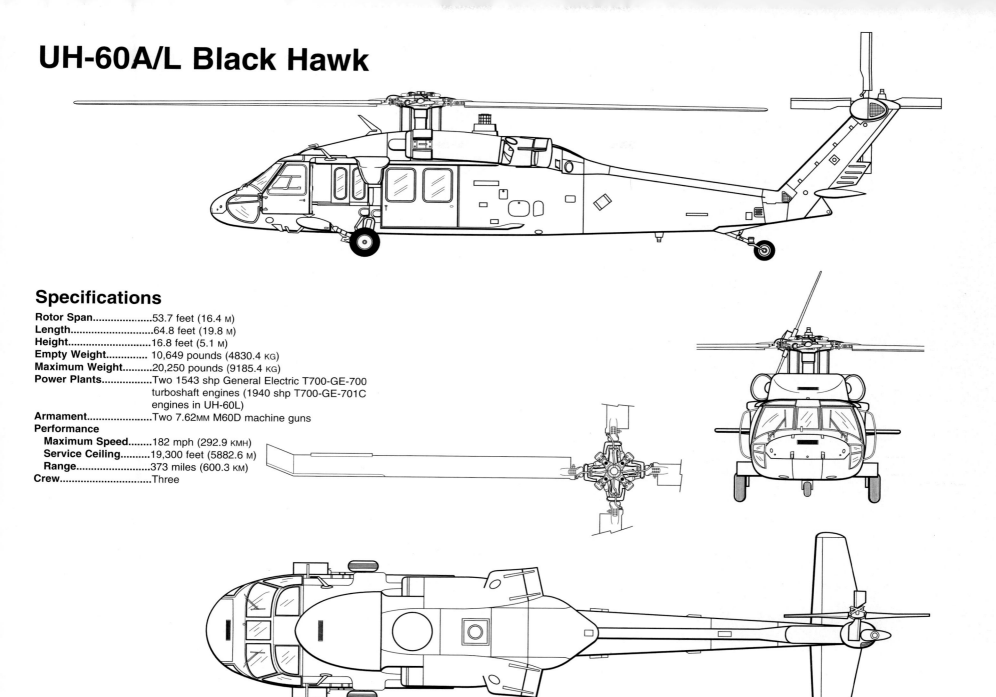

Specifications

Rotor Span....................53.7 feet (16.4 M)
Length............................64.8 feet (19.8 M)
Height............................16.8 feet (5.1 M)
Empty Weight.............. 10,649 pounds (4830.4 KG)
Maximum Weight..........20,250 pounds (9185.4 KG)
Power Plants.................Two 1543 shp General Electric T700-GE-700
                turboshaft engines (1940 shp T700-GE-701C
                engines in UH-60L)
Armament......................Two 7.62MM M60D machine guns
Performance
  Maximum Speed........182 mph (292.9 KMH)
  Service Ceiling..........19,300 feet (5882.6 M)
  Range..........................373 miles (600.3 KM)
Crew...............................Three

The main landing gear includes a drag strut running forward to the stub wing near the cockpit door and a vertical shock absorber strut. The stub wing includes a cockpit boarding step mounted in front and a position light on the outer face. Wire cutters are attached to the drag strut to split high-tension cables in the UH-60's flightpath. (Dann)

All Hawks use BF Goodrich 26 x 10.00-11 main landing gear tires with circumferential tread. The tires are inflated to a pressure of 130-140 lbs/sq in (8.96-9.65 BARS). The hydraulic brake line runs parallel to the axle strut, while the wire cutter is attached below this strut. (Dann)

This UH-60A demonstrates one of several variations to the External Stores Support System (ESSS) wing seen on Hawk variants. The removable ESSS struts are attached to the fuselage above the main landing gear. Aerodynamic fairings cover the attachment points when the ESSS is not carried. (Sherman Collings)

Fairings have been attached over the External Stores Support System (ESSS) pylon attachment fittings. The closed gunner's window is ahead of and below this fairing. The door covering the hydraulics bay access step is located beside the gunner's window. ESSS-configured UH-60s employ this access step configuration. (Dann)

The door for the hydraulics bay access step is opened allowing the step to be pulled up into position and locked in place. The hydraulics bay and flight control servos for the H-60 series are located above the cabin just forward of the main transmission. An upper tie down ring is located on the aft end of the ESSS fairing. (Dann)

The Black Hawk's main landing gear shock absorbing strut extends up the fuselage side. This early UH-60A — incapable of mounting ESSS — features a fold-down step for access to the hydraulics bay. (Dann)

The main landing gear shock absorber oleo strut is in bright, unpainted metal. The UH-60 airframe is designed to absorb an 11.25g impact with the ground before the aircraft will bottom out with the landing gear struts at full compression. A black stripe forward of the landing gear strut is a foot guide used for climbing onto the aircraft. (Dann)

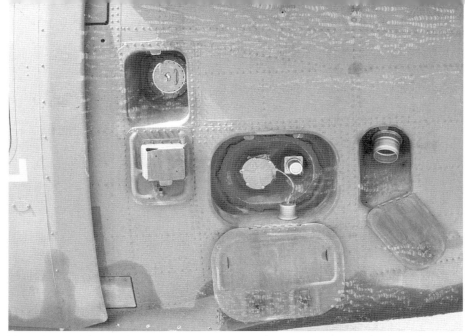

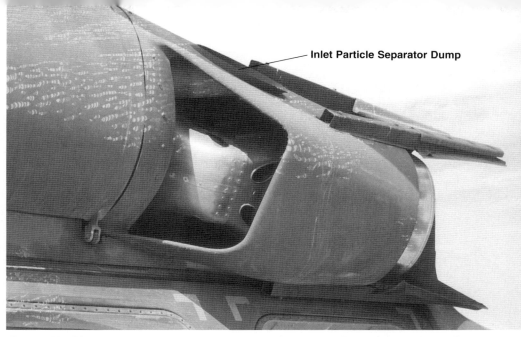

Inlet Particle Separator Dump

The red cap of the gravity fuel receptacle is located next to the port cabin door. The pressure refueling connection behind and below the gravity filler also has a red cap. Further aft is the pneumatic ground start port, which provides external air for starting the engine. All three openings are covered by access doors painted Helo Drab (FS34031). (Dann)

The Hover Infra Red Suppressor Subsystem (HIRSS) reduces the heat signature of the engines in all flight regimes by shielding the hot exhaust from direct view. Ram air entering through the front of the HIRSS provides additional exhaust cooling. The Inlet Particle Separator (IPS) dump is located on the top of the HIRSS. (Dann)

The port HIRSS exhaust assembly's natural metal surfaces are stained from heat. The IPS dump located on the top of the HIRSS expels foreign objects — such as dust — from the engine assembly to extend engine life. HIRSS was installed on all UH-60s produced after 1987 and was retrofitted to earlier Black Hawks. (Dann)

Just aft of the engine intake are the auxiliary air inlets equipped with 'blow-in' doors. These doors reduce the heat signature of the engine's forward portion. An ice detector placed between the inlet doors accumulates ice during icing conditions. Ice on this probe will trigger an ICE DETECTED caution in the cockpit. (Dann)

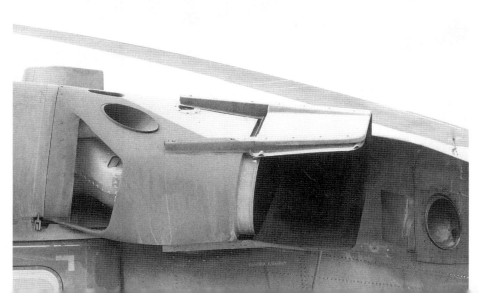

The UH-60's port pitot tube is mounted on the upper fuselage beside the hydraulic bay fairing. Another pitot tube is mounted on the starboard side of the upper fuselage. One of the aircraft's cable cutters is mounted at the front of the shroud. (Dann)

The exhaust port for the Solar T-62T-40-1 Auxiliary Power Unit (APU) is located behind the port engine exhaust. The APU can be used as an internal air source for engine start and to provide electric power for the Black Hawk through its generator. The T-62T-40-1 is mounted beside the port engine exhaust duct in the upper fuselage. (Dann)

The Sanders ALQ-144 Infrared Countermeasures (IRCM) set is located just aft of the main rotor hub. The IRCM transmitter counters heat seeking missiles by pumping out intense IR radiation at a pulsed frequency. This radiation confuses the missile's seeker head causing the missile to break lock. (Dann)

Two General Electric T-700-GE-700 engines, rated at 1543 shaft horsepower each, power the UH-60A. The Inlet Particle Separator (IPS) duct running along the engine prevents foreign objects being ingested by the engine. The hinged portion of the cowling also serves as a maintenance platform for servicing and inspection. (Dann)

The transverse stainless steel tube in the center is the pneumatic starter air duct. Bleed air from the other engine, Auxiliary Power Unit (APU), or an external air source can be used to start the engines. The IPS duct runs inboard of the engine. This is the starboard GE T-700 engine looking aft. (Dann)

The starboard Hover Infrared Suppression Subsystem (HIRSS) is mounted directly behind the engine. The Black Hawk's square Global Positioning System (GPS) antenna is mounted inboard of the exhaust. This antenna acquires navigation fixes from satellites, allowing the UH-60 to navigate with a high degree of precision. (Dann)

The main rotor tips are swept 20° aft to decrease rotor noise and increase blade efficiency. A ground adjustable trim tab is seen near the blade tip. The UH-60's rotor blades have titanium spars and are constructed primarily of fiberglass/graphite composites. Abrasion strips on the leading edges are made of titanium. (Dann)

The Black Hawk's rotor head is equipped with a bifilar vibration absorber on top to reduce rotor vibration. The blade pitch control rods attached to the rotor blade roots connect with the rotor control swash plate. The pilot alters the rotor's pitch with the collective stick. The rotor blades can be manually folded for shipping purposes. (Dann)

The UH-60's main rotor blades are painted dark gray (FS36118) with two yellow lines painted at midspan. Maintenance crews place the hoisting cuff between these lines when removing a blade, resulting in a balanced rotor blade. The Black Hawk's main rotor blades are fully articulated and are free to lead, lag, and flap during flight. (Dann)

BIM Indicator

A Blade Inspection Method (BIM) indicator is located at the square base of each blade. Rotor blades are pressurized with nitrogen and the BIM indicators will change from yellow to red should the nitrogen escape to indicate blade or spar damage. The bifilar vibration absorber on top of the main rotor hub uses weights at the end of each arm to absorb rotor vibrations. (Dann)

The pitch change rod is connected to the blade root of all H-60 Hawk variants. The de-icing control wire connects with the rotor blade leading edge. The blade damper to the right of the pitch control rod absorbs lead and lag motions during operation. (Dann)

A two-piece hinged cover on top of the aft fuselage covers the tail rotor drive shaft. The tail rotor drive shaft is built in several sections held together with 'Thomas couplings'. These couplings, similar to a U-joint, allow some flexing in the shaft, thereby reducing shaft fatigue. The two white rectangles on the spine are formation lighting strips. (Dann)

The UH-60's upper vertical fin houses a pod containing the tail rotor gearbox and tail rotor servo. The tail rotor on all H-60 versions is canted 20˚ to port and provides 2.5 percent of hover lift. A dual red/white anti-collision light is located at the top of the fin. The whip antenna is for one of the Black Hawk's two Very High Frequency/Frequency Modulation (VHF/FM) radios, which are used by Troop Commanders. (Dann)

(Left) A VHF/FM Troop Commander's radio antenna is mounted on the aft portion of the upper vertical fin. The radio for this antenna is in the cabin just above the center row of seats. A white formation light strip is located next to the anti-collision light. The upper stabilator actuator is located under the DANGER KEEP AWAY notice. (Dann)

The tail rotor on all H-60s is located on the starboard side of the vertical fin. Two paddles each of two graphite epoxy composite rotor blades are attached to a cross beam rotor hub. A pitch control spider mounted outboard of the rotor hub adjusts the rotor pitch according to input from the cockpit pedals. Tail rotor pitch is used to control yaw. (Dann)

The horizontal stabilator is controlled via a fly-by-wire system. The system determines movement based on collective position, airspeed, lateral acceleration, and pitch rate. The stabilator's movement range is 8° trailing edge up to 40° trailing edge down. Two static discharge wicks protrude from the stabilator's trailing edge. (Dann)

The intermediate gearbox redirects the tail rotor driveshaft 120° up to the tail rotor gearbox. This gearbox also provides gear reduction between the main and tail transmissions. A glass sight gauge and oil filler cap are located behind the cooling screen. (Dann)

The black tail rotor driveshaft cover also houses a VHF/FM radio antenna, and is hinged for access to the driveshaft. Painted near the leading edge of the stabilator are angle markings at -8, 0, and 40°. Just visible below the stabilator is one of four circular APR-39 radar warning antennas. There are two on the tail and two on the nose. (Dann)

The 15 x 6.00-6 tail wheel can swivel through 360° and can also be locked in the trail position. The pivot point for this wheel is at the tail wheel fork convergence point on the axle strut. The hinged main strut is attached to the airframe and shock absorber strut to absorb landing impacts. (Dann)

25

The Defensive Armed Penetrator (DAP) is a variant of the current UH-60L model designed for fire support. A 7.62MM M134 Minigun is mounted in the port gunner's window, while a 19-shot 70MM (2.75 inch) M261 Folding Fin Aerial Rocket (FFAR) pod is mounted on a shortened External Stores Support System (ESSS) wing. Six UH-60L DAP aircraft are operated by the 160th Special Operations Aviation Regiment (SOAR) at Fort Campbell, Kentucky. (Sherman Collings)

This DAP aircraft is equipped with shortened ESSS stub wings mounting a 2.75 inch (70MM) rocket pod. A red port position light is located on the stub wing tip. A retractable rope ladder is attached to the top of the cabin for troop insertions. (Sherman Collings)

The starboard side of this same DAP Black Hawk has another M134 Minigun in the crew chief's window. The General Electric 7.62MM M134 is a six-barreled weapon capable of firing from 2000 to 4000 rounds per minute. This gun entered service during the later half of the 1960s on UH-1C Hueys deployed as gunships to Vietnam. The M134 Minigun, including its drive, is 42.88 in (108.9 CM) long and weighs 67 lbs (30.4 KG). (Sherman Collings)

This DAP Black Hawk is equipped with a Hughes 30MM M230 Chain Gun on the starboard ESSS wing. The M230 can fire between 600 and 650 rounds per minute. A green position light is located on the stub wing tip, and an M134 Minigun is mounted in the gunner's window. (Sherman Collings)

The Honeywell Volcano mine dispensing system is a recent addition to the UH-60's weapons capabilities. Volcano consists of two mounts of 80 mine canisters mounted in each cabin door, for a total capacity of 160 mines per aircraft. (Sherman Collings)

(Right) The Volcano dispenser forward mounting mechanism is located just behind the gunner's window. A support strut with a foot pad is attached to the landing gear stub wing and the Volcano's mounting rack. The mount is painted Helo Drab (FS34031) while the mine launcher is painted light green, believed to be FS34583. (Sherman Collings)

Light blue (believed to be FS35466) inert rounds are mounted on this Volcano mine dispenser. The stenciling on the mine rounds is in white. The mines are launched out and away from the Black Hawk. (Sherman Collings)

The MH-60K Special Operations Aircraft prototype conducts a test flight. The undersurfaces and tail boom are painted gray, various panels are covered in chromate primer, and the rest of the airframe is painted Helo Drab (FS34031). The MH-60K is the latest addition to the US Army's 160th Special Operations Aviation Regiment, based at Fort Campbell, Kentucky. Based on the UH-60A aircraft, the MH-60K incorporates an in-flight refueling probe, a nose-mounted APQ-174 Multi-Mode Radar, and an AAQ-16 Forward Looking Infrared (FLIR) turret mounted below the radar. This aircraft also features the folding stabilator, main rotor brake, and Automatic Flight Control System (AFCS) of the US Navy SH-60B Seahawk. A total of 57 antennas are mounted on the MH-60K's airframe. (Sikorsky via Sherman Collings)

An AAR-47 missile warning receiver is mounted on the MH-60K's port stub wing, below the cockpit door. The crew access step below the receiver was redesigned from the UH-60A's step to minimize wire strike effects. The upper half of the red position light is blacked out to reduce excess light when flying on night vision goggles. (Jim Rotramel via Sherman Collings)

The MH-60K's ARN-118 TACAN (Tactical Air Navigation) blade antenna is mounted on the spine of the aircraft. An M130 chaff/flare dispenser is mounted on the fuselage next to ARMY. Below STATES is the Bendix/King ARN-123 VOR (VHF Omni Range)/Localizer antenna. VOR is the civilian equivalent to the military TACAN and is used for airways navigation and instrument approach procedures. (Jim Rotramel via Sherman Collings)

The External Stores Support System (ESSS) wings on the MH-60K are upswept to allow a greater field of fire for the cabin mounted 7.62mm M134 Miniguns. A 230 gallon (870.6 LITER) external fuel tank is mounted on the wing. A green starboard position light has been fitted to the tip of the ESSS wing. (Jim Rotramel via Sherman Collings)

(Above) The MH-60K's primary recognition feature is the nose fairing for the Texas Instruments APQ-174 Multi-Mode Radar, which possesses terrain following capability. The Hughes AAQ-16 FLIR is located beneath the nose. Two screens on the nose cowl flanking the APQ-174 provide cooling for the large amount of mission electronics. The Identification Friend or Foe (IFF) blade antenna is mounted next to the port cooling screen. (Jim Rotramel via Sherman Collings)

(Above Left) The MH-60K cockpit includes an Electronic Instrumentation System (EIS). The two outboard instrument panel Multi-Function Displays (MFDs) use monochrome (green) screens while the two inboard MFDs are in color. The Forward Looking Infrared (FLIR) turret control grip is mounted on the center console. (Jim Rotramel via Sherman Collings)

(Left) Two small black E-Systems APR-39 pulse radar-warning antennas are located on the MH-60K's nose cowl. Above these antennas are small fairings for the radar beacon antenna on the starboard side of the aircraft and the IFF antenna on the port side. An AAR-47 missile warning receiver is mounted on the starboard side of the In-Flight Refueling (IFR) probe, opposite the silver IFR light. A rectangular Instrument Landing System (ILS) glideslope antenna is mounted immediately below the radar dome and a small Northrop Grumman ALQ-36 Electronic Support Measures (ESM) antenna is located under the ILS. The FLIR turret is mounted under the nose. (Jim Rotramel via Sherman Collings)

The UH-60Q DUSTOFF (Dedicated Unhesitating Service To Our Fighting Forces) is the Army's newest Medical Evacuation (MEDEVAC) helicopter. The aircraft is equipped with a chin mounted Forward Looking Infrared (FLIR), weather radar, satellite communications, and the Global Positioning System (GPS). The UH-60Q is also equipped with state-of-the-art medical equipment including an oxygen generation system (MSOGS), an Intravenous (IV) solutions warmer/cooler unit, and space for up to six litters. (Sikorsky via Bill Tuttle)

UH-60Q

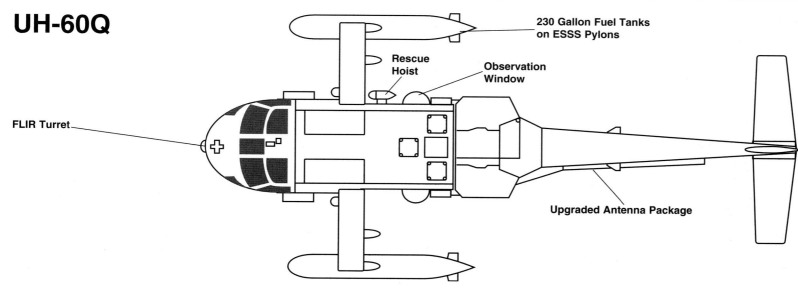

230 Gallon Fuel Tanks
on ESSS Pylons

Rescue
Hoist

Observation
Window

FLIR Turret

Upgraded Antenna Package

(Above) A Forward Looking Infrared (FLIR) turret is located under the nose of the UH-60Q. Two hand holds are located next to the radio compartment access door fasteners. The small black disk on the hatch is one of the Black Hawk's APR-39 pulse radar warning antennas. (Sherman Collings)

(Above Left) Two 230 gallon (870.6 LITER) external fuel tanks are attached to the UH-60Q's External Stores Support System (ESSS) pylons. The aircraft is equipped with the latest tactical navigation and communication equipment, allowing the UH-60Q to perform aeromedical evacuation missions under extremely hostile conditions. (Sherman Collings)

(Left) The UH-60Q cabin interior is configured to carry up to six litter patients. The litters are mounted on vertical rails along the sides of the cabin. These litters can be moved up or down as necessary. Seating for ambulatory patients can also be carried. (Sherman Collings)

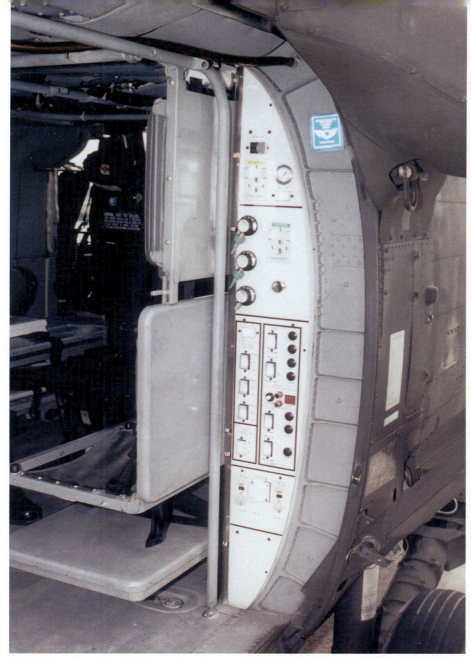

Medical equipment control panels are mounted in the starboard cabin doorway. These panels include (from top): 28 volt Direct Current power supply and air units, oxygen system controls with three knobs, litter lift controls, and 115/220 volt Alternating Current power supply. Next to the doorway are the ESSS pylon support struts. (Sherman Collings)

The medical cabinet is placed against the rear cabin bulkhead. At the top of the cabinet is the oxygen system control panel, while two warmer/cooler Intravenous (IV) solutions units are located at the center. The rest of the cabin consists of supply drawers. (Sherman Collings)

Antenna Arrangement
UH-60/EH-60

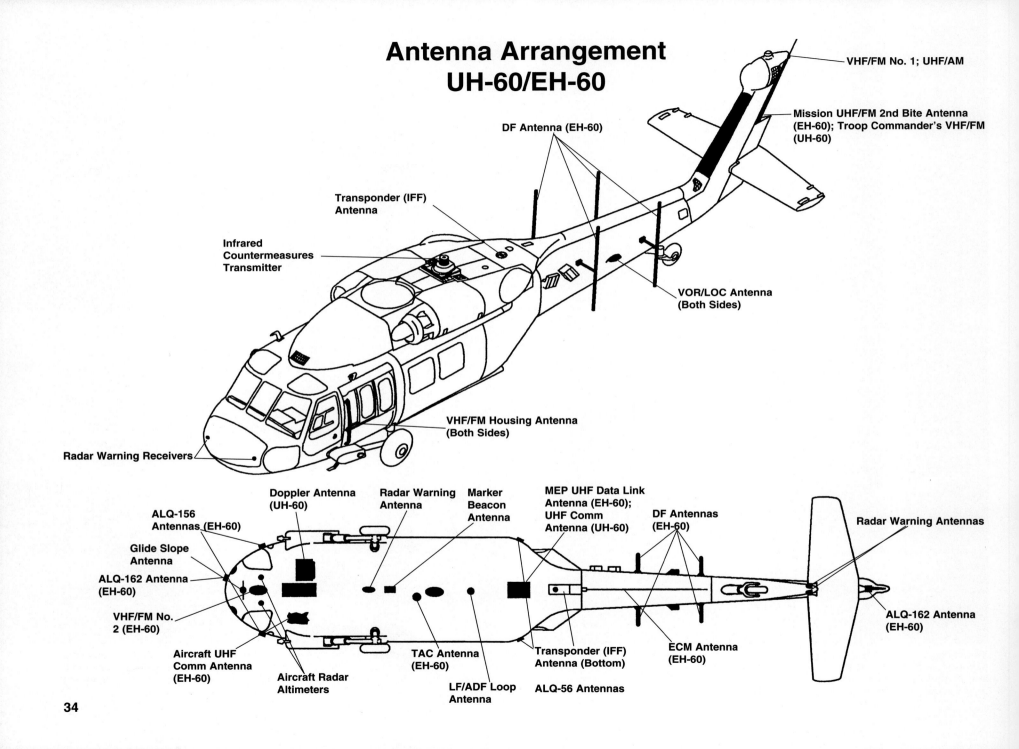

VHF/FM No. 1; UHF/AM

Mission UHF/FM 2nd Bite Antenna (EH-60); Troop Commander's VHF/FM (UH-60)

DF Antenna (EH-60)

Transponder (IFF) Antenna

Infrared Countermeasures Transmitter

VOR/LOC Antenna (Both Sides)

VHF/FM Housing Antenna (Both Sides)

Radar Warning Receivers

Doppler Antenna (UH-60)

Radar Warning Antenna

Marker Beacon Antenna

MEP UHF Data Link Antenna (EH-60); UHF Comm Antenna (UH-60)

DF Antennas (EH-60)

Radar Warning Antennas

ALQ-156 Antennas (EH-60)

Glide Slope Antenna

ALQ-162 Antenna (EH-60)

VHF/FM No. 2 (EH-60)

Aircraft UHF Comm Antenna (EH-60)

Aircraft Radar Altimeters

TAC Antenna (EH-60)

LF/ADF Loop Antenna

Transponder (IFF) Antenna (Bottom)

ALQ-56 Antennas

ECM Antenna (EH-60)

ALQ-162 Antenna (EH-60)

34

The EH-60A Quick Fix conversion was an attempt to provide the US Army with a battlefield electronic interception, monitoring, and jamming platform. The aircraft is equipped with a large retractable Electronic Counter Measures (ECM) antenna below the fuselage and four Direction Finding (DF) antennas on the aft fuselage. This EH-60A prototype was superceded by the operational EH-60C. The Army received 66 EH-60Cs equipped with ESSS mounts, the Hover Infrared Suppressor Subsystem, and a wire strike kit. (Sikorsky)

The starboard landing light extended under the nose is fitted with an Infrared (IR) lens. An identical light is located under the port nose. With the IR lens in place, only personnel wearing night vision goggles can see the light. A guide for the wire strike protection kit is placed under the pilot's door. (Dann)

The whip antenna mounted on the nose compartment is used by National Guard UH-60s to communicate with civilian agencies, such as police and firefighting personnel. The APR-39 threat warning receiver is located just forward of the antenna. One of the two latches securing the nose compartment hatch is further forward. (Dann)

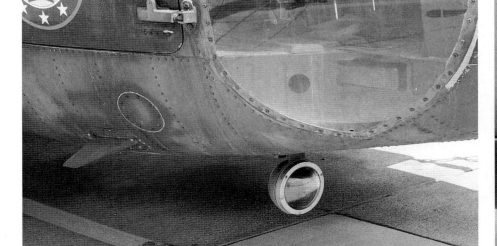

USAF HH-60G Pave Hawk

The US Air Force operates the MH-60G Pave Hawk for combat rescue and special operations support missions. This aircraft is based on the UH-60A/L, however, the Pave Hawk incorporates an in-flight refueling probe, radar, and a Forward Looking Infrared (FLIR) turret on the nose. The MH-60G is capable of night and all-weather operations. The USAF operates 16 MH-60Gs for special operations missions and an additional 82 HH-60G rescue aircraft. The HH-60G lacks the FLIR turret and the External Stores Support System (ESSS) pylons that are standard on the MH-60G.

(Below) A radome positioned on the port side of the nose houses a Bendix/King 1400C color weather/mapping radar. The 55th Special Operations Squadron based at Hurlburt Field, Florida is the primary operator of the MH-60G. (Dann)

(Above) The US Air Force Special Operations Command (AFSOC) operates the MH-60G Pave Hawk. The Pave Hawk incorporates an in-flight refueling probe, a nose mounted radar, and a folding stabilator. (Sikorsky via Bill Tuttle)

(Below) The MH-60G can be equipped with the AAQ-16 Forward Looking Infrared (FLIR) unit under the nose. The Hughes AAQ-16 is displayed in the stowed position. The MH-60A, K, and L also use this FLIR. (Dann)

An in-flight refueling probe is installed on the starboard side of the MH-60G's nose. The boom's forward telescoping portion extends approximately nine feet (2.7 METERS) to allow the boom to clear the helicopter's rotor arc for refueling operations. (Sherman Collings)

(Right) The cockpit of the MH-60G is similar to that of the UH-60L except for mission specific equipment. This equipment includes the radar display visible above the port cyclic stick. The Pave Hawk cockpit is equipped with analog flight instruments. (Sherman Collings)

The in-flight refueling probe is faired into the HH-60G's starboard stub wing. The cockpit boarding step mounted on the stub wing has been redesigned to accommodate the probe. The HH-60G lacks the nose mounted FLIR turret and provision for ESSS pylons of the MH-60G. (Sherman Collings)

The in-flight refueling probe is attached to the MH-60G's starboard stub wing. The silver in-flight refueling light is mounted in a fairing next to the downward vision window. The black circular item above the light is an APR-39 pulse radar warning antenna. (Sherman Collings)

The tip of the in-flight refueling (IFR) probe fits into the drogue trailed by the tanker aircraft. IFR-equipped Black Hawks and Pave Hawks are capable of refueling from HC/KC-130 Hercules aircraft. This capability allows IFR-equipped helicopters to self-deploy overseas. (Sherman Collings)

MH-60G Pave Hawk

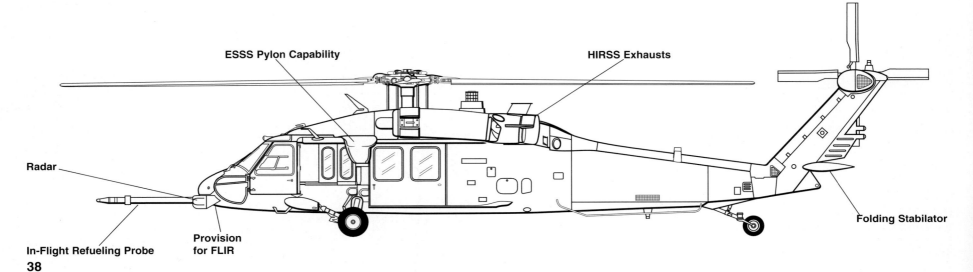

ESSS Pylon Capability

HIRSS Exhausts

Radar

In-Flight Refueling Probe

Provision for FLIR

Folding Stabilator

38

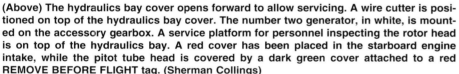

(Above) The hydraulics bay cover opens forward to allow servicing. A wire cutter is positioned on top of the hydraulics bay cover. The number two generator, in white, is mounted on the accessory gearbox. A service platform for personnel inspecting the rotor head is on top of the hydraulics bay. A red cover has been placed in the starboard engine intake, while the pitot tube head is covered by a dark green cover attached to a red REMOVE BEFORE FLIGHT tag. (Sherman Collings)

(Above Right) The Pave Hawk's main rotor hub is the same as that for the UH-60. A pitch control rod connects each rotor blade root with the rotor control swash plate. Bifilar vibration dampeners are fitted between each rotor root to reduce vibration to the helicopter. A white Blade Inspection Method (BIM) indicator is mounted at the rotor blade root. This indicator lets Pave Hawk maintenance crews know if pressurized nitrogen has been lost from the blades. A loss of charge indicates possible compromise of blade structural integrity.

(Right) The MH-60G Pave Hawk is equipped with External Stores Support System (ESSS) pylons. Red port position lights are mounted on both the tip of the pylon and on the landing gear attachment stub wing. The starboard ESSS wing and landing gear stub wing have green position lights. A stores rack and sway braces are attached to the outboard pylon on the ESSS wing. A static discharge wick is attached to the aft wingtip. (Sherman Collings)

Some Pave Hawks are equipped with this older internal rescue hoist kit, which pivots on its vertical post for proper positioning. This hoist is a self-contained unit except for airframe electrical power. Most MH-60Gs are equipped with the same rescue hoist used on the US Navy SH-60B Seahawk. (Sherman Collings)

(Left) The MH-60G is armed with two General Electric 7.62mm M134 Miniguns, one in each gunner's window. This six-barreled weapon can fire at either 2000 or 4000 rounds per minute. A spent shell chute is attached to the Minigun's breech. (Dann)

This MH-60G is equipped with a Robertson internal auxiliary fuel tank system in the rear of the cabin. These are held in place using tie-down straps. Each of the two cells fitted can hold 185 gallons (700.3 LITERS). Fuel distribution lines are located on top of the tank. (Sherman Collings)

During OPERATION DESERT STORM in 1991, some Air Force HH-60Gs were repainted in Tan (FS30400) and Earth (FS30140). All markings were in black. (Sherman Collings)

The interior of the MH-60G Pave Hawk is similar to that of the Army's UH-60L. The gunners sit behind the pilots in the forward cabin, each gunner's seat facing the window. The interior is painted light gray (FS36375) with olive drab (FS34087) soundproofing material. (Sherman Collings)

The US Air Force deployed the MH-60G Pave Hawk rescue helicopter to Saudi Arabia for OPERATION DESERT STORM during 1991. The Pave Hawks employed during the war were camouflaged in Tan (FS30400) and Earth (FS30140). The USAF security policeman in the foreground is wearing the now obsolete 'chocolate chip cookie' desert camouflage uniform. (USAF)

Turnbuckles attach the cabin seats to a support structure on the cabin ceiling. Two red fittings on the ceiling are used to attach rappelling rope hooks. (Sherman Collings)

41

The H-60 Hawk family was designed and built for ease of maintenance. The opened engine cowlings also serve as engine servicing platforms. Maintenance crewmen can stand on a small platform in the hydraulics bay when inspecting the flight control system and rotor head. Red intake and exhaust covers are fitted in place with red REMOVE BEFORE FLIGHT streamers attached to the covers. (Sherman Collings)

A technician stands on the port engine cowling while inspecting the top of the HH-60G. The large white device next to the serviceman's boot is a generator. A hydraulic pump is located just forward of the generator. (Sherman Collings)

Cold air is mixed with hot engine exhaust through the inner baffles of the Hover Infrared Suppressor System (HIRSS). The cooler exhaust air is further dissipated by the rotor downwash to reduce the aircraft's heat signature. HIRSS is now found on nearly all Air Force and Army Hawks. HIRSS's lack of moving parts reduces maintenance on the assembly. (Dann)

The fuel dump on the HH-60G Pave Hawk is located on the starboard side of the fuselage near the aft tie down ring. The system will dump fuel at a rate of over 800 lbs (362.9 KG) per minute. The dump is painted light gray, believed to be FS36320. (Dann)

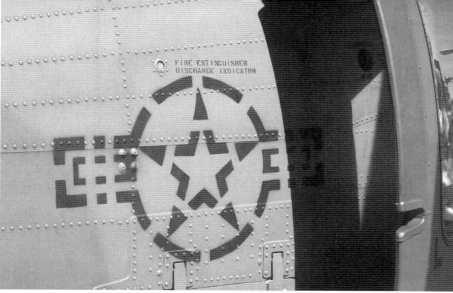

Air Force Pave Hawks use this low-visibility black star for the national insignia. The small red disc above the insignia is the fire extinguisher thermal discharge plug. This plug will blow out if there is a thermal overpressure of the engine fire extinguisher system. (Dann)

(Right) The Pave Hawk is equipped with black Tracor M-130 chaff/flare dispensers on either side of the fuselage which can be quickly removed from the aircraft. Each of the 30 cells holds one chaff or flare round. This particular dispenser is used for chaff and is pointed upward. When used for flares, the M-130 is mounted to release flares downward. (Dann)

Air Force MH-60s use the same rescue hoist as the Navy's SH-60s. This light gray (FS36375) hoist is taken from a Seahawk. The rescue hoist is capable of lifting 600 lbs (272 KG), and is powered by the aircraft's backup hydraulic system. Personnel are advised to not touch the pendant until it touches the ground or water to avoid static electrical shock generated by the helicopter. (Dann)

US Navy SH-60B/F Seahawk

The SH-60B was developed from the UH-60A Black Hawk to fulfill the US Navy's requirement for a second generation LAMPS (Light Airborne Multipurpose System) helicopter to succeed the Kaman SH-2. The LAMPS helicopter was designed to perform anti-submarine warfare (ASW) and surface attack missions. The SH-60B is designed to operate from smaller US Navy ships and is equipped with power folding rotor blades and a manually folding tail boom to facilitate on board stowage. The SH-60B Seahawk entered service during 1983, and 165 of the 210 SH-60Bs requested by the Navy have entered service.

The SH-60F Ocean Hawk is a SH-60B modified for the inner zone — within the escort ships' screen — ASW role on board aircraft carriers. A total of 76 SH-60Fs were produced. The Navy plans to modify existing SH-60Bs and SH-60Fs to SH-60R standard in the future. The SH-60R combines the capabilities of the SH-60B with the SH-60F's dipping sonar. Other SH-60B derivatives include 37 HH-60H Rescue Hawk combat rescue and covert operations aircraft.

'Red Stinger 103', an SH-60B attached to HSL-49, taxis out of the flight line at NAS North Island in San Diego, California. This Seahawk carries the Middle East Force (MEF) modification, which includes Tracor ALE-39 chaff and flare dispensers on either side of the aft fuselage and provisions for two Sanders ALQ-144 infrared countermeasures sets: one aft of the main rotor and the other forward of the tail wheel. Four ALQ-156 threat warning receivers are installed, with one each on the nose and tail, and the other two just aft of the pilots' doors. A 7.62MM M-60 machine gun is mounted in the cabin door. (US Navy)

Two square Raytheon ALQ-142 Electronic Sensor Measures (ESM) antennas flank a Sierra Research ARQ-44 data link antenna on the SH-60B's nose. ESM is used to identify emitter sources, such as radar. Two pitot tubes are mounted near the chin windows to collect airspeed data. (Dann)

The nose equipment bay of the Seahawk houses avionics equipment. The forward TACAN (Tactical Air Navigation) antenna is mounted in the nose cowl. REMOVE BEFORE FLIGHT flags cover each pitot tube when the aircraft is parked. (Dann)

44

Steadying the wild beast! This SH-60B (BuNo 162339) slipped in the Rapid Securing Device (RSD) of USS CURTS (FFG-38) and nearly tipped over during a deployment off the coast of Japan in September of 1988. The starboard tire is about one foot (0.3 M) off the flight deck. This incident occurred while the helicopter maintenance detachment was aligning the Seahawk with the Recovery Assist Secure and Traverse (RAST) track (in foreground) while readying the SH-60B for hangar stowage. (Jeff Merrick)

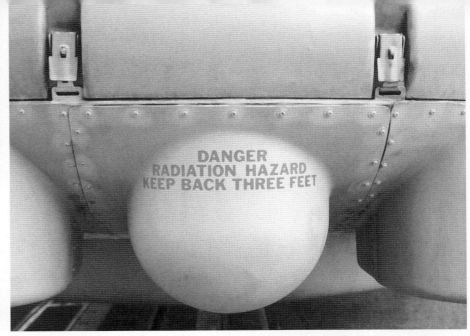

A recent addition to the Seahawk is the addition of FLIR/Hellfire capability. Seventy-eight SH-60Bs and HH-60Hs will have the AAS-44 Forward Looking Infrared (FLIR) turret mounted on the nose and four AGM-114A Hellfire missiles mounted on the port outboard stores rack. The FLIR turret will include a laser designator to allow the Seahawk to designate their own targets. The remainder of the Seahawk fleet will be modified to carry a FLIR turret on the starboard stores rack as a kit, but will not carry Hellfires. (Dann)

The forward antenna for the ALQ-44 data link is mounted in the SH-60B's nose. This two-way digital duplex data link, known as 'Hawklink', allows the aircrew to relay secure voice, raw radar video, and tactical information to the parent ship. With FLIR capability being added to the SH-60B, infrared images will also be relayed to the host ship. (Dann)

SH-60B Seahawk

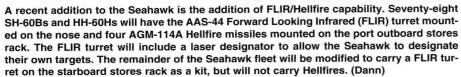

ALQ-142 ESM

ALQ-142 ESM

APS-124 Surface Search Radar

Sonobuoy Launcher

Aft ALQ-44 Data Link Antenna

SH-60B Seahawk

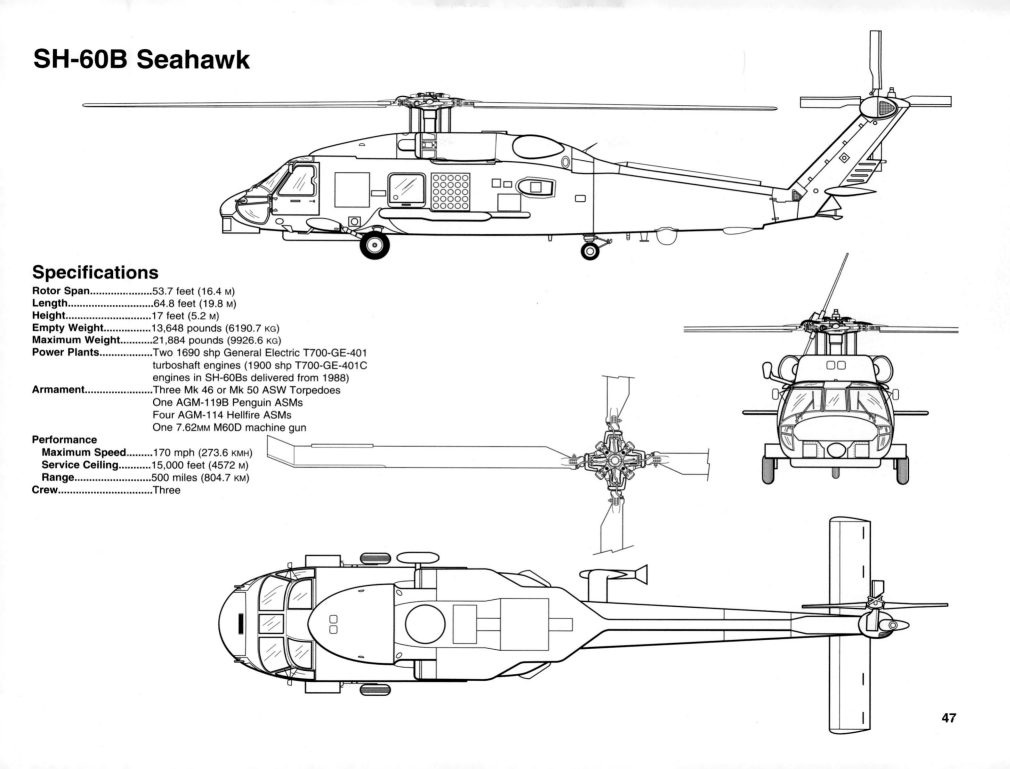

Specifications

Rotor Span....................53.7 feet (16.4 м)
Length............................64.8 feet (19.8 м)
Height...........................17 feet (5.2 м)
Empty Weight...............13,648 pounds (6190.7 кg)
Maximum Weight..........21,884 pounds (9926.6 кg)
Power Plants.................Two 1690 shp General Electric T700-GE-401
turboshaft engines (1900 shp T700-GE-401C
engines in SH-60Bs delivered from 1988)
Armament.......................Three Mk 46 or Mk 50 ASW Torpedoes
One AGM-119B Penguin ASMs
Four AGM-114 Hellfire ASMs
One 7.62мм M60D machine gun

Performance
  Maximum Speed.........170 mph (273.6 кмн)
  Service Ceiling...........15,000 feet (4572 м)
  Range.........................500 miles (804.7 км)
Crew...............................Three

The Airborne Tactical Operator (ATO) in the SH-60B's port seat supervises the tactical scenario while the Pilot in the starboard seat flies the aircraft. Both pilots are fully qualified to fly in either seat. The seats are covered with sheepskin and are equipped with five-point buckles and lumbar supports. (Raatz)

Engine instruments on the left side of the Pilot's instrument cluster show temperatures, pressures, torque, and RPM. Flight instruments on the top row are (L to R): the airspeed indicator, attitude indicator, and radar altimeter. The barometric altimeter is located just below the latter. Other flight instruments line the bottom of the cluster. (Raatz)

The port Airborne Tactical Officer's door of the SH-60B includes a window, which can be jettisoned in case of ditching. The yellow handle on the door is the window emergency release. This window lacks the small sliding portion found on Army and Air Force H-60s. A rear view mirror is located to the right of the door. The SH-60 is air-conditioned and on humid days clouds of condensation fill the cockpit! (Dann)

The Sensor Operator (SO) station is located in the port side of the cabin. The SO — an enlisted crewmen in the Aviation Systems Warfare Operator (AW) rating — is responsible for running mission sensors. AWs are also Search And Rescue (SAR) qualified swimmers. Two AWs are carried on a SAR mission, one to run mission systems, and the other will go into the water if necessary. (DP Associates via Tracy Kreckman)

The RAST (Recover Assist, Secure, and Traverse) probe is housed in the aft portion of the cabin. The RAST system was developed to facilitate deck handling of helicopters. Standard on the SH-60B, this system can be used by SH-60F and H models. (Raatz)

The sonobuoy launcher is located behind the Sensor Operator's station. Sonobuoys are launched using high pressure air fed from a manifold through the silver tubes. The RAST main probe, used for shipborne landings in heavy seas, is mounted under the launcher. The Sensor Operator (SO) is in charge of operating both acoustic and non-acoustic sensors. (Dann)

49

The center of the Sensor Operator's (SO) console features a Multi-Purpose Display (MPD). Surrounding the MPD are controls for tuning sonobuoys, deploying the Magnetic Anomaly Detector (MAD), monitoring Electronic Sensor Measures (ESM), and operating the radar. (DP Associates via Tracy Kreckman)

An observer or aircrew seat is located in the aft starboard corner of the cabin. Hoist controls are located on the grip on the wall and on the long cord along the wall. Using the wall grip, the aircrewman under 'crew hover' control can maneuver the Seahawk in any direction at speeds up to five knots (9.3 кмн). (DP Associates via Tracy Kreckman)

The SH-60B's sonobuoy launcher is capable of carrying 25 sonobuoys, but cannot be reloaded in flight. Nineteen buoys are loaded on this Seahawk's launcher. The SH-60B can carry both passive and active sonobuoys, as well as chaff buoys. Buoys are launched by means of a compressed air charge through a manifold. An exercise Mk 46 torpedo hangs from the port inboard stores rack. (Dann)

SH-60B Seats

Pilot's Seat

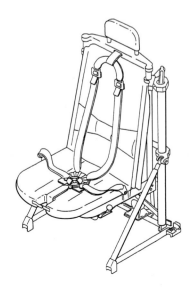

Passenger's Seat

SH-60B (BuNo 162991) demonstrates the tail fold arrangement of the Seahawk family. The outer portions of the stabilator are manually folded up, while the tail pylon folds to port. This photo was taken aboard the cruiser USS MOBILE BAY (CG-53) during OPERATION DESERT STORM in 1991. (Dann)

When not carrying sonobuoys, a simple aluminum panel covers the launcher. This cover is a favorite of squadron artists. The Rapid Securing Device (RSD) below the SH-60B allows the helicopter to recover in heavy seas, and moves aircraft into the hangar with minimal human interaction. (Dann)

The SH-60 series vertical landing gear strut is approximately two feet (0.6 M) tall and attached to the lower fuselage. The starboard stub wing has a green position light and a step for the pilot. The stub wing housed flotation bags when they were installed, however, these bags were removed due to ditching hazards they posed for the crew. (Dann)

The starboard avionics cooling fan is located just aft of the stub wing. Stenciling near the fan is in dark gray (FS36320). Another cooling fan is located on the port side near the landing gear stub wing. The starboard wheel brake line runs down the landing gear strut. (Dann)

The starboard electronic junction box access door is decorated with an HSL-43 squadron insignia. Two static ports located just forward of the access door measure static air pressure for such instruments as the barometric altimeter and airspeed indicator. The hinged ring above the door is used to tie the aircraft down on deck in heavy seas. (Dann)

The access door has been opened to reveal the starboard electrical junction box, located just aft of the cockpit. The generator control units and bus tie relays are located in this box. A recessed step to the left allows maintenance personnel to reach and service the hydraulics bay. (Dann)

Two SH-60Bs — rotors, stabilators, and tail folded — are stowed in the ship's hangar. The tail rotor drive shaft is located in the fairing on top of the aft fuselage. The red bar below the pylon fold is a tool used to manually fold the pylon. An extension is inserted into the tool's end and used by the deck crew to swing the tail into position. (Dann)

An ALQ-142 Electronic Support Measures (ESM) antenna is mounted on the starboard fuselage under the engine exhaust. This is one of four ESM antennas — two forward and two aft — giving 360° of coverage and allowing the Seahawk to identify radar emitters. The wire surrounding the ESM antenna is the High Frequency (HF) radio antenna. (Dann)

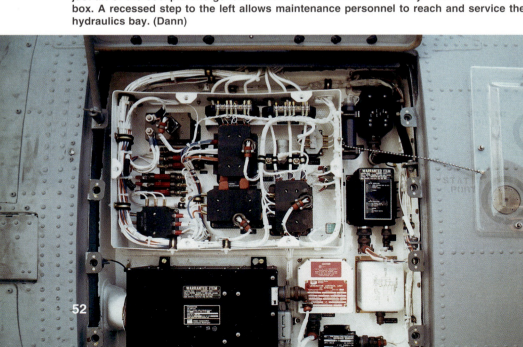

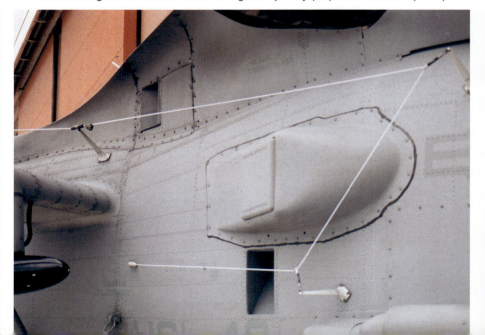

The SH-60B is equipped with a Texas Instruments AQS-81 Magnetic Anomaly Detection (MAD) set mounted on the starboard side of the aircraft. The MAD 'bird' is trailed on a cable 200 feet (60.9 M) behind the aircraft and is used to detect disturbances in the earth's magnetic field. Large ferrous objects — such as submarines — can cause these disturbances. (Dann)

A Sierra Research ARQ-44 data link antenna is mounted on the lower aft fuselage. The lower Very High Frequency (VHF)/Ultra High Frequency (UHF)/Tactical Air Navigation (TACAN) antenna is located just forward of the ARQ-44 antenna. (Dann)

SH-60 series main rotor blades are held secure by the use of blade crutches when in the folded position. Clamps at the end of each crutch are attached to the blades. The tube along the spine of the aircraft is the tail rotor drive shaft. (Dann)

The Seahawk tailwheel was moved some 13 feet (3.96 M) forward from that of the Black Hawk to facilitate shipboard landings. This wheel is fully castoring, however, it can be locked in the trail position for running landings and shipboard operations. The fuel dump tube is to the tailwheel's right. (Dann)

The H-60 Hawk series tail rotor is constructed of two graphite composite paddles crossed at the center. Pitch control rods directly twist the tail rotors to change rotor pitch, rather than through bearings as employed by most helicopters. This important feature eliminates the need to grease tail rotor bearings, thus reducing maintenance time. Retractable steps along the vertical fin allow the crew to inspect the tail rotor gearbox. (Dann)

The tail rotor on the Seahawk/Black Hawk helicopter family is a tractor type and is mounted 20° from vertical. This mount allows the tail rotor to provide 2.5% of hover lift. The vertical fin is offset slightly to starboard. The upper actuator at the base of the vertical fin is used to position the stabilator, which on SH-60 Seahawks has a range of 8° (forward flight) to 40° (hover) trailing edge down. (Dann)

(Above) Tail rotor pitch is changed through in and out movement of the pitch control shaft. Pitch change rods at the rotor hub twist the blades as the shaft moves out. Small electrical connectors at the base of each blade are part of the blade de-icing system. Heating elements running the length of the leading edge soften ice forming on the rotors, which adversely affects flight characteristics. (Dann)

(Above Right) The SH-60's stabilator folds manually for hangar stowage. The folded stabilator is kept in place by a small 'crutch' installed by the deck crew. The small circular object near the stabilator root is a retractable step used by maintenance crews to inspect the tail rotor. The tail pylon is folded after the stabilator has been folded. With the rotors and tail rotor folded, the SH-60B's length of 64.8 ft (19.8M) is reduced to 40.9 ft (12.5M). (Dann)

(Right) A tail skid located at the base of the Seahawk's tail is designed to keep the stabilator from impacting the ground in extreme nose-high attitudes. Just above the tail skid is the stabilator fold joint. The stabilator is part of the aircraft's fly-by-wire control system and ranges in elevation from 8° trailing edge up to 40° trailing edge down. (Dann)

An SH-60B equipped with an AGM-119 Penguin air-to-surface missile prepares to land aboard USS HALYBURTON (FFG-40) during Penguin integration testing. This aircraft is performing a Recovery Assist (RA) landing, and the ship's RA cable is attached to the air- craft's RAST (Recovery Assist Secure and Traverse) main probe. This unique system allows the SH-60B to land even when the ship is rolling up to 15° and pitching up to 4°. (Kurt Long via Pete Kover)

(Below) The Honeywell and Gould Mk 46 Mod 5 torpedo is the current standard aircraft and surface launched torpedo in the US Navy. This torpedo weighs 507.1 pounds (230 KG), including a 97 pound (44 KG) warhead. (Dann)

(Above) Saberhawk 71, an SH-60B assigned to HSL-47, drops a Mk 46 exercise torpedo off the coast of San Diego, California. The torpedo's stabilizing chute has begun to deploy. Orange cameras mounted above the main landing gear strut and on the aft fuselage were used to photograph this test launch sequence. (DP Associates)

(Below) The SH-60B/F can carry up to three Mk 46 Mod 5 torpedoes, two on the port side and one on the starboard side. The Mk 46 is an acoustic homing torpedo with counter-rotating screws. The orange object at the rear of the torpedo is a parachute, which both slows and aligns the weapon prior to water entry. (Dann)

The Honeywell Mk 50 Barracuda torpedo is the newest anti-submarine warfare (ASW) weapon to be carried by the SH-60 family. This particular Mk 50 is a training shape, which allows the deck crew to familiarize themselves with loading and unloading. The torpedo is attached to a BRU-14A bomb rack on the Seahawk's starboard side. (Dann)

In an effort to expand the offensive capabilities of the SH-60B, a number of aircraft were modified to carry the Kongsberg AGM-119B Penguin anti-ship missile. The Norwegian-developed missile is carried on a special pylon, and has folding fins for proper clearance aboard ship. Blue trim indicates a practice missile. (Hanxleden)

The Penguin anti-ship missile is ten feet (3.1 M) long with a diameter of 11 inches (27.9 CM). Gross weight of the AGM-119B is 847 pounds (384.2 KG), and the missile's warhead weighs 265 pounds (120.2 KG). The missile's maximum range is approximately 30 nautical miles (55.5 KM). Penguin is an infra-red homing missile with inertial guidance. (Hanxleden)

BRU-14A Bomb Rack

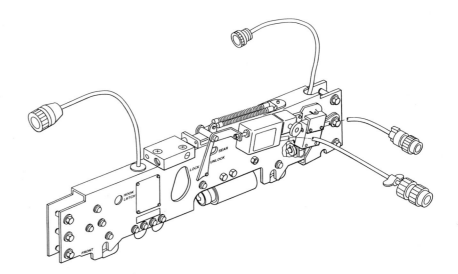

This SH-60F is assigned to Helicopter Anti-Submarine Squadron Ten (HS-10), the West Coast SH-60F Fleet Replacement Squadron. A High Frequency (HF) wire antenna is mounted on the rear fuselage. The fuselage staining is caused by exhaust from the starboard 1900 HP General Electric T-700-401C engine. All Seahawk variants have a cabin door on the starboard side only. A small, spring-loaded auxiliary door allows the cabin door to slide past the starboard weapon pylon. The SH-60's main rotor turns at a maximum rate of 258 RPM. (DP Associates)

SH-60F Seahawk

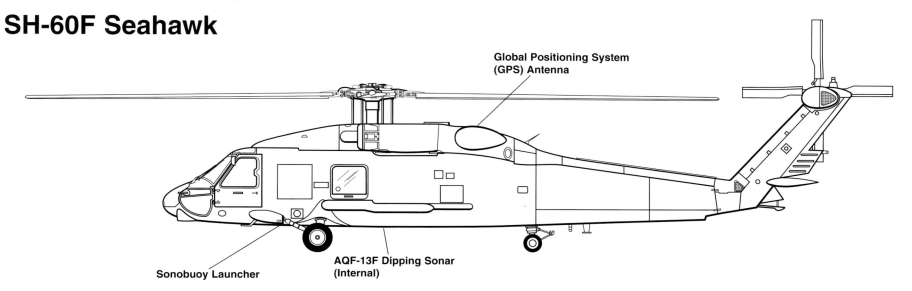

Global Positioning System (GPS) Antenna

Sonobuoy Launcher

AQF-13F Dipping Sonar (Internal)

The covers have been removed from the BRU-14A bomb rack on this SH-60F. Up to three weapon stations may be mounted on the Seahawk. This rack is used by all Seahawk variants. A 120 gallon (454.2 LITER) auxiliary fuel tank is attached to the inboard rack. Anti-Submarine Warfare (ASW) torpedoes may also be carried on these racks. (Dann)

Radar altimeter antennas are mounted in fairings under the nose of the SH-60F. The gun-like protuberance near the chin bubble is the starboard pitot tube. Rear view mirrors are located just forward of the pilots' doors. A cockpit boarding step is located on the forward portion of the stub wing. (Dann)

The hydraulics bay for all H-60 variants is located above the cockpit and is housed under a sliding 'doghouse' cover. This area houses all hydraulic pumps, generators, and flight control servos for the aircraft. Two static ports are located just forward of the HS-8 'Eightballer' squadron emblem. At the time of this photo, HS-8 was preparing for a deployment onboard the aircraft carrier USS NIMITZ (CVN-68). (Dann)

The open access doors on the port rear fuselage of an SH-60F reveal (from left): Cabin equipment, gravity refueling receptacle, pressure refueling panel, ARC-182 VHF radios, and pneumatic ground start port. (Dann)

The six round sonobuoy launcher is nestled into the lower fuselage between the landing gear stub wings. The dark square further aft is the cargo hook cutout. The dome just aft of the cargo hook houses the On Top Position Indicator (OTPI), which allows the crew to locate deployed sonobuoys. A cable has been deployed from the rescue hoist. (Rodd Mullett)

(Right) The Seahawk can carry a 7.62MM M60 machine gun — capable of firing 600 rounds per minute — on a swivel mount in the cabin door. The ammunition box to the gun's left carries 550 rounds. A spent cartridge box is mounted to the right of the M60. This gun mount is generally seen on SH-60B and F models. (Dann)

An aircrewman prepares to bring a rescued person aboard a Helicopter Anti-Submarine Squadron 10 SH-60F. The aircrewman holds the rescue hoist 'pendant', which contains hoist controls. The rescue hoist is used by all naval H-60 variants, and is capable of holding up to 600 pounds (272.2 KG). (Rodd Mullett)

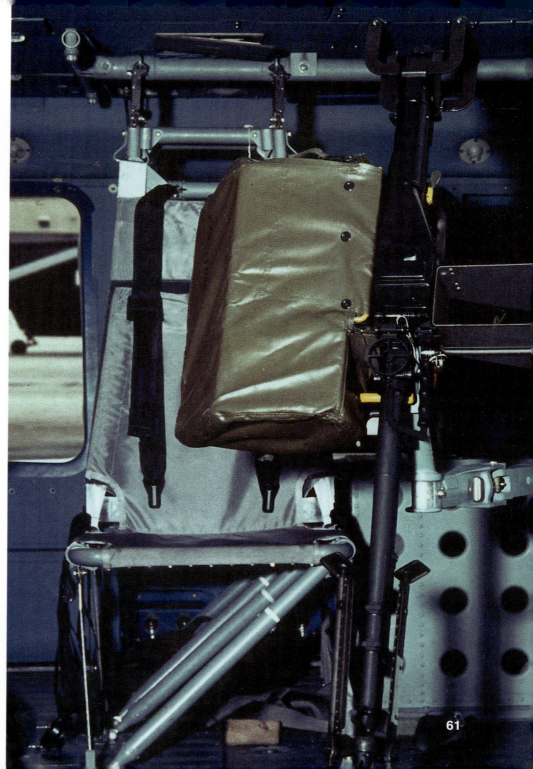

The TSO console is displayed in the stowed position. The TSO console consists of a Multi-Function Display (MFD), a Control Display Unit (CDU, the upper keyset) and the Display Control Panel (DCP, the lower keyset). The entire upper half of this unit (with the MFD, CDU, and DCP) slides to the left in front of the TSO seat. (DP Associates via Tracy Kreckman)

The Tactical Systems Operator (TSO) is seated at his console in the SH-60F's cabin. The console is deployed in the unstowed position in front of the TSO. The Acoustic Sensor Operator (ASO) is in the background working on his equipment. (DP Associates via Tracy Kreckman)

The sonar reeling machine and an observer's seat are located in the aft area of the SH-60F's cabin. The sonar transducer is stowed in its cylindrical enclosure in the center of the cabin. The ASO console is in the background at right. (DP Associates via Tracy Kreckman)

The SH-60F is capable of carrying 14 active or passive sonobuoys. Six are loaded into the launcher, while another eight are stored in the adjacent carousel. The flight crew manually loads the sonobuoys into the launcher. The SH-60F acoustic processing system can process both passive and active sonobuoys. (Dann)

The Acoustic Sensor Operator (ASO) reads sonar returns on the Azimuth/Range Indicator (ARI, the round scope). The Sonar Data Computer (SDC) is located below the ARI. A Control Display Unit (CDU) is located to the left of the SDC control panel, while various controls are placed above the CDU. (DP Associates via Tracy Kreckman)

The SH-60F's primary mission sensor is the Bendix AQS-13F dipping sonar. The transducer is stored within the clear plastic housing in the cabin. Next to this housing is the sonar reeling machine, which stores the 1500 feet (457.2 m) of cable used to deploy the transducer. (Dann)

The main rotor blades are attached to the hub by means of a spindle assembly. The spindle's 'elastomeric bearing' allows for lead, lag, and flapping motion to occur. The circular objects to the left are the bladefold lockpin motors. A droop stop located on the rotor hub, above the rear view mirror, prevents excessive rotor drooping at low RPM. (Dann)

The swashplate at the base of the main rotor mast transmits flight control inputs to the main rotor via the four pitch control rods surrounding the mast. A band on the control rod corresponds to the rotor blade's assigned color: red, yellow, blue, or black. A light located forward and right of the main rotor illuminates droop stops. (Dann)

The Environmental Control System (ECS) is positioned just aft of the main rotor hub beside the Auxiliary Power Unit (APU). The ECS provides air conditioning for the crew and avionics cooling in the nose bay and in the 'transition' section behind the fuel tank. Air from engine bleed or the APU powers the ECS. (Dann)

The inlet particle separator located left of the starboard engine prevents foreign objects from being ingested into the engine. The engine accessory section is located at the front of the powerplant. The hydromechanical unit located to the left of the starter housing is used to meter the appropriate amount of fuel for engine operation. (Dann)

The yellow oil filler cap is at the bottom left of this view of the same engine looking aft. The cylinder at lower right is the oil filter bypass. The silver tube running over the engine supplies air to the pneumatic starter. Two T700-GE-401 engines each rated at 1690 shaft horsepower (SHP) powered SH-60Bs delivered before 1988. Two 1900 SHP T700-GE-401C engines power SH-60s delivered from 1988 and were retrofitted to older aircraft. (Dann)

An HH-60H Rescue Hawk from Reserve Helicopter Combat Support Squadron Five (HCS-5) flies near a frigate in the Pacific Ocean. The Rescue Hawk is fitted with the Hover Infrared Suppressor Subsystem (HIRSS) over the exhausts to reduce IR signature. HCS-5, based at NAS Point Mugu, California, is one of two reserve squadrons operating the HH-60H, the other being HCS-4 at NAS Norfolk, Virginia. The HH-60H Rescue Hawk is a combat rescue and covert operations aircraft based on the SH-60F airframe. The US Navy received 45 Rescue Hawks for deployment with the two reserve units and the SH-60F squadrons. Helicopter Antisubmarine (HS) squadrons embarked on aircraft carriers include two HH-60Hs with four SH-60Fs. The HH-60H can also fitted with Recovery Assist Secure and Traverse (RAST) equipment to allow deployment on various vessels. The Rescue Hawk was employed on rescue and covert missions during OPERATION DESERT STORM in 1991. (US Navy)

HH-60H Rescue Hawk

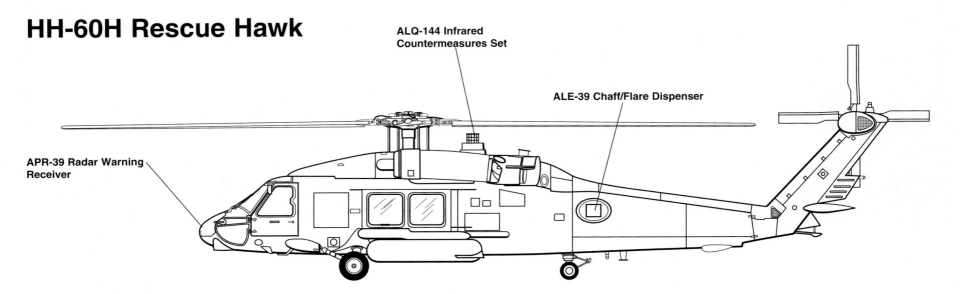

ALQ-144 Infrared Countermeasures Set

ALE-39 Chaff/Flare Dispenser

APR-39 Radar Warning Receiver

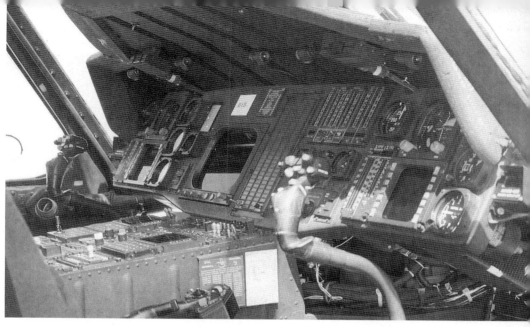

The nose of the HH-60H has been modified to include cable cutters on the nose, the main landing gear struts, and the hydraulics bay 'doghouse' on the upper fuselage. The rear view mirrors have been moved downward to just above the door hinge. Antennas for the Downed Aircrew Locator System (DALS) are located beneath the fuselage. The black discs near the pitot tubes are the APR-39 Radar Warning Receivers. (Dann)

The HH-60H is equipped with two port side sliding windows. The aircraft can carry one 7.62MM M60D machine gun in the starboard cargo door and another in the forward port-side window. Alternatively, 7.62MM GAU-17 Gatling guns can be mounted. The outboard pylon and bomb rack have been removed from this HH-60H. (Dann)

The large Multi-Function Display (MFD) screen at the center of the HH-60H instrument panel is used to view the tactical scenario. Inputs to the MFD are made with a keyset and cursor located on the center console — an arrangement common to all Seahawk variants. The HH-60H cockpit is Night Vision Goggle (NVG) compatible, employing blue lighting instead of the standard red cockpit lighting. (Dann)

One of the primary recognition features of the HH-60H is the faired Tracor ALE-39 chaff and flare dispenser. When the ALE-39 is used, the cover is removed and the flares and chaff cartridges are loaded into individual cells. Another recognition feature is the HIRSS over the exhaust to reduce the IR signature at all flight regimes. (Dann)

H-60 Hawks are equipped with two cyclic sticks, which allow either pilot to fly the aircraft. There are numerous controls on the cyclic stick, including the guarded emergency release switch on the stick grip top. This switch releases equipment attached to the helicopter by cable — RAST, cargo hook, MAD, sonar or hoist. The red trigger switch is the radio/inter-communications system transmitter control. (Dann)

(Left) The center console of the HH-60J is similar in appearance to those of the US Navy's SH-60F and HH-60H. Two keypads, known as Control Display Units (CDUs), allow the pilots to make inputs to the Multi-Function Display (MFD) at the upper left. To the right of the MFD is the caution and warning panel. Automatic approach/hover controls are located between the CDUs. (Dann)

The layout of the HH-60J's primary flight instrument cluster is similar to all Seahawk models, although the B models have an analog BDHI (Bearing Distance Heading Indicator). Later Seahawks feature a digital HSVD (Horizontal Situation Video Display). (Dann)

The overhead panel contains controls for the engine, Auxiliary Power Unit (APU), and aircraft lighting. The large handle with the red knob is the rotor brake, which quickly slows down the rotor. The throttle quadrant houses the fire extinguisher 'T' handles, fuel control levers (gray knobs), and Power Control Levers (PCL) with starter buttons. (Dann)

The HH-60J collective pitch stick grip includes several switches common to other Seahawks. Among these are a searchlight control, a heading trim switch, collective trim trigger, a flight control servo shutoff switch, and a contingency power switch. (Dann)

The overhead console on the Seahawk series includes a circuit breaker panel above the co-pilot's seat. The Power Control Levers (PCLs) are in the forward center of the overhead. Engine start buttons are located on each PCL. The circuit breaker panel gives the co-pilot's overhead window a unique shape. (Dann)

The 'rudder' pedals control the pitch of the tail rotor. Yaw trim switches are located on the heel of the pedal. Pushing the tops of the 'rudder' pedals activates the wheel brakes, a function similar to fixed wing aircraft. (Dann)

US Coast Guard HH-60J Jayhawk

The US Coast Guard's HH-60J Jayhawk is a medium range recovery helicopter based on the Navy's SH-60F Seahawk. The Jayhawk is equipped with a search/weather radar in the nose, and may be fitted with a nose mounted Forward Looking Infrared (FLIR) turret. The HH-60J is capable of flying 300 miles (482.8 KM), loitering for one and a half hours, and returning with six passengers. Alternatively, this aircraft can loiter for one and a half hours while performing law enforcement missions. The Jayhawk can operate from HAMILTON and BEAR Class cutters, in addition to shore bases. The Coast Guard received 35 Jayhawks between 1990 and 1993 for deployment at Coast Guard Air Stations across the country.

The HH-60J Jayhawk is a medium range Search And Rescue (SAR) variant of the Seahawk developed for the US Coast Guard. This aircraft is based on the SH-60F airframe, however, the Jayhawk features a nose mounted RDR-1300C search/weather radar. The Jayhawk carries two 120 gallon (454.2 LITER) fuel tanks on the port stores rack, and can carry an additional fuel tank on the starboard stores. In addition to SAR duties, the HH-60J is employed on law enforcement tasks. These tasks include drug interdiction, anti-smuggling patrols, and surveillance and protection of the environment. (Sikorsky)

The most distinctive feature on the HH-60J Jayhawk is the radome for the Bendix/King RDR-1300C search/weather radar. The Jayhawk can also carry a Forward Looking Infrared (FLIR) turret beneath the fuselage and just aft of the radome. Coast Guard Jayhawks are without a doubt the most colorful H-60s anywhere. (Dann)

Fairings flanking the radome house the HH-60J's radar altimeter antennas. The two probes just forward of the center windshield are outside air temperature probes. The pitot tubes are located on either side of the nose. They are positioned at slightly different angles, with the port pitot pointing slightly downward. (Dann)

The external configuration of the HH-60J is similar to that of the HH-60H, with the cabin door on the starboard side and two sliding windows on the port side. The forward window slides forward while the rear window slides aft. (Dann)

The High Frequency (HF) radio antenna is rigged differently on the Jayhawk versus other naval H-60 variants. At the extreme left is the tail pylon fold line. The tail is manually folded and stows along the port side of the fuselage. (Dann)

The HH-60J tail pylon assembly is identical to that of the SH-60B Seahawk and its derivatives. When being folded for shipboard storage, the tail swings 180° to lay against the port fuselage. Inside the folding tail assembly are the tail rotor drive shaft and servo hydraulic lines. (Dann)

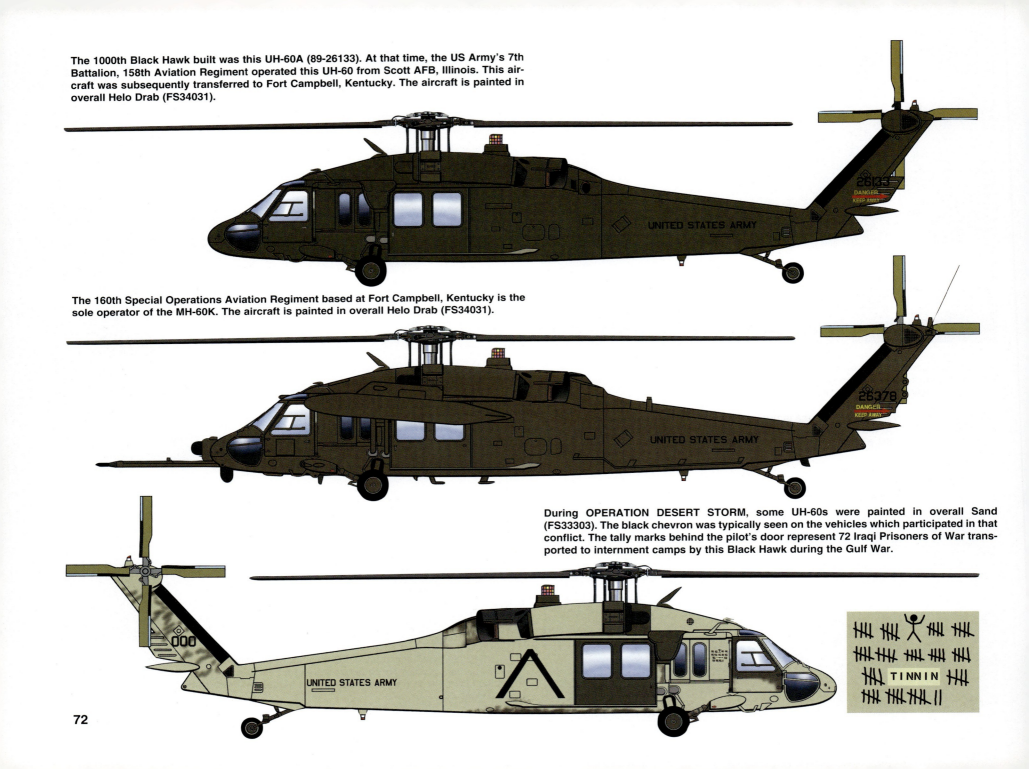

The 1000th Black Hawk built was this UH-60A (89-26133). At that time, the US Army's 7th Battalion, 158th Aviation Regiment operated this UH-60 from Scott AFB, Illinois. This aircraft was subsequently transferred to Fort Campbell, Kentucky. The aircraft is painted in overall Helo Drab (FS34031).

The 160th Special Operations Aviation Regiment based at Fort Campbell, Kentucky is the sole operator of the MH-60K. The aircraft is painted in overall Helo Drab (FS34031).

During OPERATION DESERT STORM, some UH-60s were painted in overall Sand (FS33303). The black chevron was typically seen on the vehicles which participated in that conflict. The tally marks behind the pilot's door represent 72 Iraqi Prisoners of War transported to internment camps by this Black Hawk during the Gulf War.

USAF MH-60G Pave Hawks such as this one of the 55th Special Operations Squadron at Eglin Air Force Base's Hurlburt Field, Florida are painted in Dark Green (FS34102), Medium Green (FS 34092), and Gray (FS36231).

Several 55th Special Operations Squadron MH-60G Pave Hawks were painted Tan (FS 30400) and Earth (FS30140) prior to deployment to the Persian Gulf for OPERATIONS DESERT SHIELD/DESERT STORM.

Some 55th SOS MH-60G Pave Hawks based at Hurlburt Field have recently been repainted in overall Gunship Gray (FS36118).

An early production UH-60A Black Hawk was marked with the Red Cross on a white square on the cabin doors and nose. This marking indicated the helicopter's role as a Medical Evacuation (MEDEVAC) aircraft. Early UH-60s were not equipped to carry ESSS pylons and HIRSS exhaust kits. The US Army is replacing UH-60As assigned to MEDEVAC missions with purpose-built UH-60Qs. (Manfred Faber)

A UH-60A carries a 105mm M102 howitzer to a new firing position during OPERATION DESERT STORM in 1991. Black Hawks were extensively used during the conflict with Iraq, allowing US Army units to rapidly deploy and strike from bases miles away from the fighting. (USAF via Cole)

This MEDEVAC UH-60A has the main rotor blades folded to facilitate shipment aboard a transport aircraft. Temporary struts secure the manually folded rotors to the aft fuselage. Two of the Black Hawk's crew sits beside the open cabin door, while a third crewman services the tail rotor. (Manfred Faber)

This HIRSS-equipped UH-60A returned from Persian Gulf service in 1991 still wearing its overall Sand (FS33303) camouflage scheme except where the paint has worn off. All markings are in black, including a Coalition force identification chevron aft of the main cabin. The markings behind the pilot's door represent 72 Iraqi prisoners of war transported to internment camps by this Black Hawk. (Werner Roth)

An early production UH-60A back from OPERATION DESERT STORM displays little weathering to the temporary Sand camouflage scheme. A UH-60 in overall Helo Drab (FS34031) and wearing a yellow chevron is parked in the background. US forces lost six UH/SH-60s during the Gulf War — two to enemy action and the remainder to accidents. (Werner Roth)

A SH-60B Seahawk hovers above the flight deck of the cruiser USS PHILIPPINE SEA (CG-58), while a crewman in the cabin pulls up the rescue hoist. The USS PHILIPPINE SEA was deployed to the Persian Gulf during OPERATION DESERT SHIELD, the US deployment to protect Saudi Arabia from Iraqi attack between 2 August 1990 and 16 January 1991. (US Navy by CWO Ed Bailey)

One of five prototype SH-60B Seahawks is parked on the ramp at Naval Air Station Patuxent River, Maryland during US Navy testing in the early 1980s. The Seahawk was painted flat white on the upper surfaces and sides, while the under surfaces were painted gloss Light Gray (FS16440). An SH-3 — the type the SH-60F would replace on board aircraft carriers — is parked next to the Seahawk. (Gerhard Weinmann)

The HH-60J Jayhawk is the Coast Guard's primary medium range rescue helicopter. The Coast Guard received 35 HH-60Js between 1990 and 1993 for operation from bases across the United States. The Jayhawk is also employed on anti-drug and environmental surveillance missions. (P. Fiegel)

SH-60B Seahawk (BuNo 162991) of HSL-43 was one of the first Navy Seahawks modified with the FLIR/Hellfire conversion. This is the same aircraft flown by the author during OPERATIONS DESERT SHIELD/DESERT STORM in 1990/91. The color scheme is Dark Gray (FS36320) upper surfaces, Light Gray (FS36375) sides, and Light Gray (FS36495) under surfaces.

This SH-60B Seahawk was assigned to HSL-51 'Warlords' at Naval Air Facility Atsugi, Japan during 1999. The Seahawk's aft fuselage has been decorated with a rising sun and Mount Fuji motif, while a samurai warrior derived from the squadron emblem has been painted on the tail.

Navy directives currently allow one aircraft per squadron to be painted brightly. These are commonly referred to as 'CAG (Commander Air Group) Birds'. This SH-60F (BuNo 164075) is assigned to Helicopter Anti-Submarine Squadron 4 (HS-4) at NAS North Island, California.

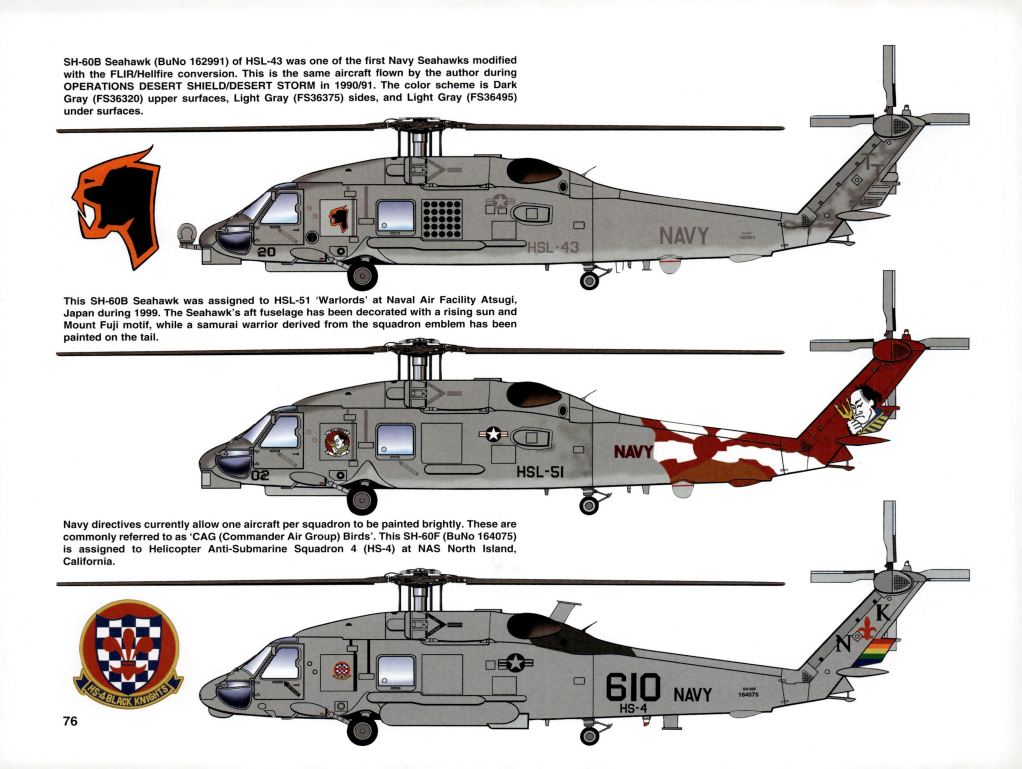

This all Black SH-60F (BuNo 164092) is one of several assigned to the Naval Strike and Air Warfare Center (NSAWC) at NAS Fallon, Nevada. The insignia on the forward fuselage combines the lightning bolt of Strike U with the emblem of Top Gun.

This SH-60F (BuNo 164089) is assigned to the NSAWC at NAS Fallon. The aircraft is painted Desert Tan (FS33531) and Brown (FS30118) with a Light Ghost Gray (FS36440) bottom.

This HH-60J is assigned to Coast Guard Station San Diego. The aircraft is painted in overall Insignia White (FS 17875) with International Orange (FS 12197). This aircraft has a FLIR turret mounted under the nose. The FLIR is a kit installation and can be removed and installed on other aircraft.

77

The author prepares to land aboard the aircraft carrier USS MIDWAY (CV-41) during operations in the Persian Gulf in OPERATION DESERT STORM. Forward visibility is somewhat restricted by the instrument panel glareshield. (LT Scott Giffin)

A Horizon Reference System (HRS) light bar, located near the lower right corner of the SPY-1A radar antenna, assists the pilot during night approaches. This gyrostabilized device helps the pilot maintain a level attitude when hovering over the flight deck. The Stabilized Glideslope Indicator (SGSI) left of the HRS gives final approach glideslope information in the form of a green, amber, or red light. The far right red, amber, and green deck status lights are used to clear the pilot for takeoff and landing. (Dann)

A Full Scale Development SH-60B hovers during flight deck compatibility testing aboard an OLIVER HAZZARD PERRY Class Frigate. The Recovery Assist Secure and Traverse (RAST) system cable is in hover tension (approximately 2000 lbs/907.2 KG). The pilot will then lower his hover to about four feet (1.2 M) and wait for the appropriate moment to land. Once the pilot calls 'ready to land', the Landing Signal Officer (in the LSO shack to the left) will apply 4000 lbs (1814.4 KG) of tension to the cable. Once landed, hydraulic jaws on deck will capture the RAST probe located on the bottom of the helicopter. (Sikorsky)

The flight deck of the destroyer USS OLDENDORF (DDG-972) is an integral part of the SH-60B Light Airborne Multi-Purpose System (LAMPS). The line down the center of the deck is the line-up line for approach to the flight deck. The circle ensures that the aircraft will have proper rotor clearance with the hangar if the SH-60's main wheels are inside the circle. Two sets of left/right line-up lines are painted on the hangar door, one for each Rapid Securing Device (RSD), the trolley-like device within the circle. The two sets of hash marks serve as fore/aft line-up lines. The RSD (there are typically two on ships) moves in and out of the hangar under the command of the Landing Safety Officer (LSO). Operating from the LSO shack (upper right of picture), he assists the flight crew using voice calls and deck status lights. The LSO also manipulates the RAST controls. (Terry Richie)

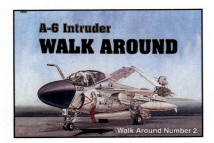

5502 A-6 Intruder

5503 F-14 Tomcat

5504 F4F Wildcat

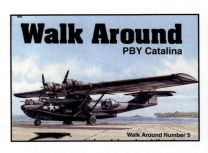

5505 PBY Catalina

5506 B-52 Stratofortress

5508 P-40 Warhawk

5510 Fw 190D

5511 P-47 Thunderbolt

5512 B-25 Mitchell

5513 Allison Engined Mustangs

5514 Hurricane

5515 Mosquito

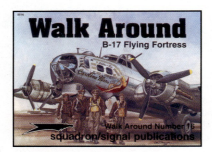

5516 B-17 Flying Fortress

5517 A-10 Warthog

5518 F/A-18 Hornet

5520 Space Shuttle